THE AFFIRMATIONS DOT-TO-DOT PUZZLE BOOK

THE AFFIRMATIONS DOT-TO-DOT
PUZZLE BOOK

Compiled by
Patience Coster

SIRIUS

SIRIUS

This edition published in 2019 by Sirius Publishing, a division of
Arcturus Publishing Limited,
26/27 Bickels Yard, 151–153 Bermondsey Street,
London SE1 3HA

Copyright © Arcturus Holdings Limited

ISBN: 978-1-78888-770-0
CH006755UK

Printed in China

Introduction

How can you best achieve a happy, positive outlook on life while exercising your brain at the same time? The dot-to-dot puzzles in this book promise a great mental workout, while affirmative quotes encourage an optimistic, reflective way of thinking. With symbols, animals, plants, and patterns inspired by meditation and spiritual healing, there is something here for everyone to enjoy.

All you need to start are a sharp pencil and a ruler (for the bigger spaces between dots). Take care to follow the correct numerical sequence – this can be tricky, as the numbers are not always positioned next to one another.

Take your time, and meditate on each completed image. Allow the quotes and affirmations to make you think more deeply. You will be surprised at the sense of positivity and achievement you derive from this pastime. We hope you have fun joining the dots, completing the pictures, and mulling over the words of the wise.

I have fun with all
of my endeavours,
even the most mundane.

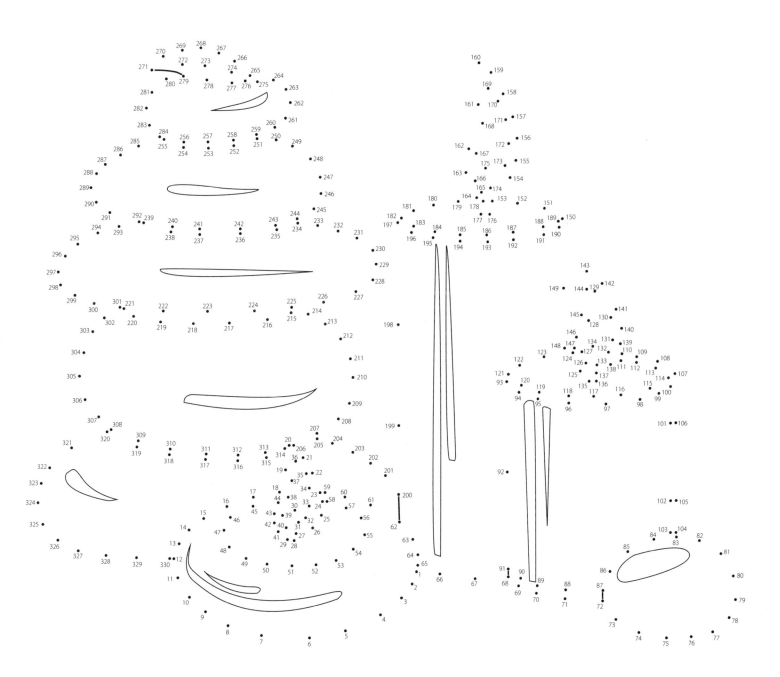

'The ones who are crazy enough
to think they can change the world
are the ones who do.'

Steve Jobs

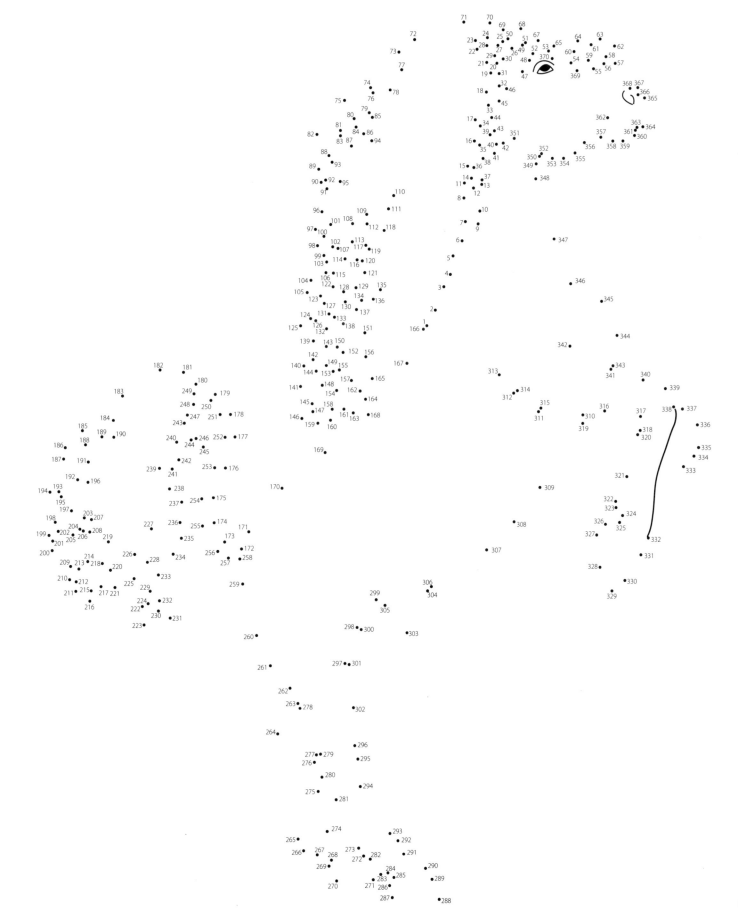

I have healthy boundaries with my partner, family and friends.

I am

and I am

§§§

'I am not a product of
my circumstances.
I am a product of my decisions.'

Stephen Covey

§§§

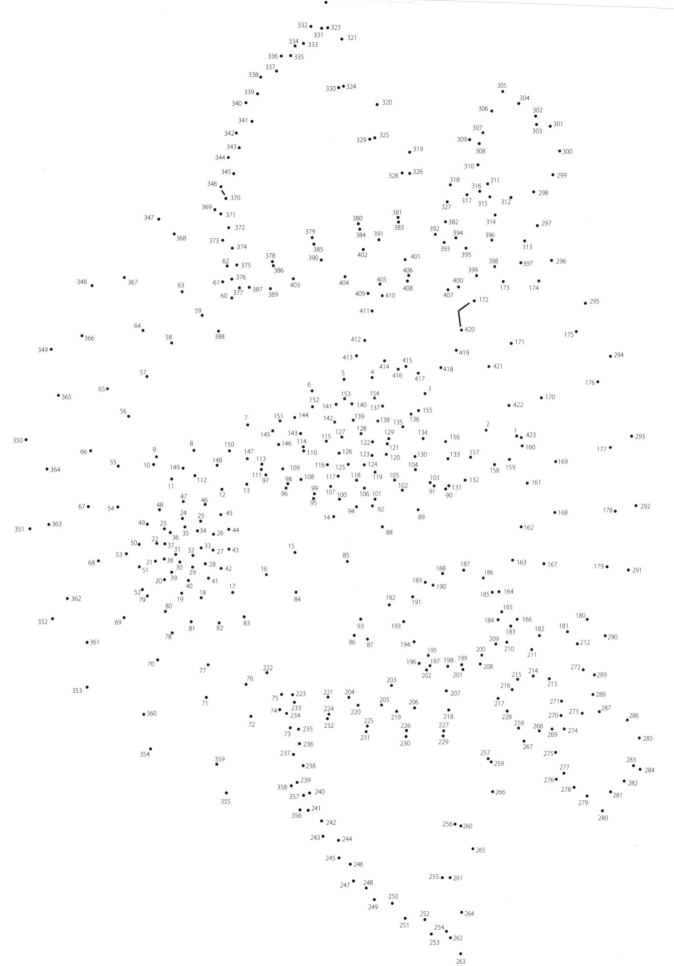

I view mistakes and setbacks
as stepping stones to my success.

I am

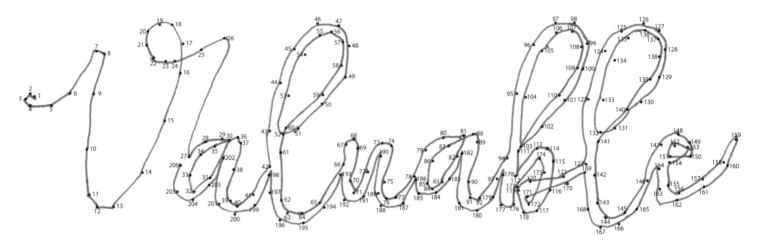

and my efforts are

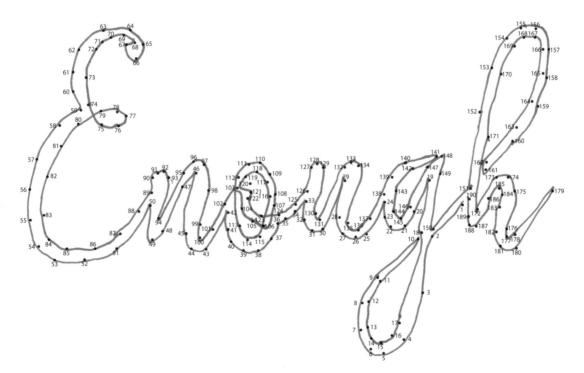

'You are never too old
to set another goal
or dream a new dream.'

C.S. Lewis

I easily find solutions to challenges
and move onwards quickly.

I have

accomplished

much to be

of

§§§

'I have found that among its other benefits, giving liberates the soul of the giver.'

Maya Angelou

§§§

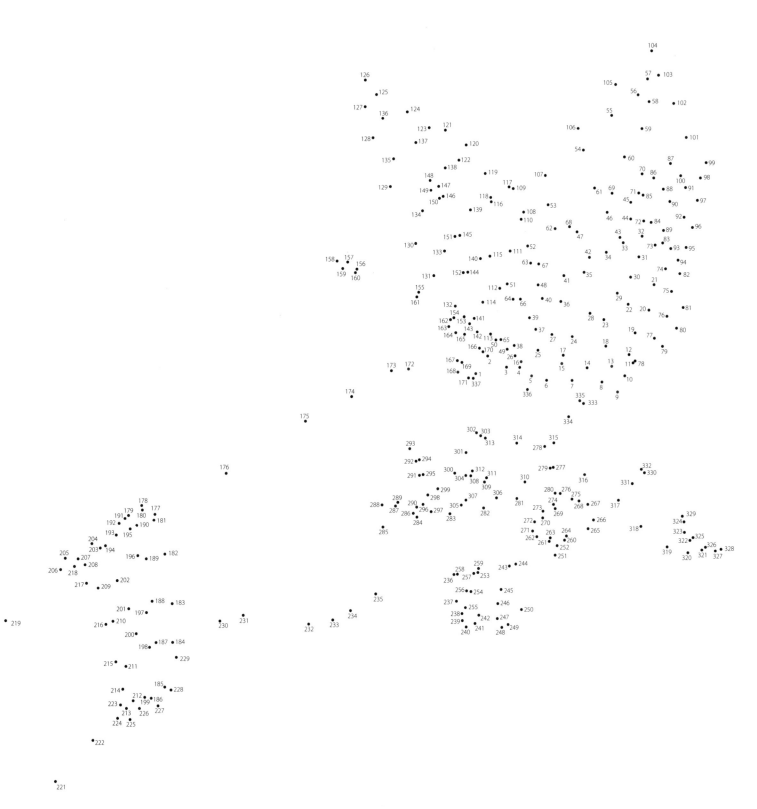

*I live in the present
and am confident of the future.*

'Your self-worth is determined by you. You don't have to depend on someone telling you who you are.'

Beyoncé

I am

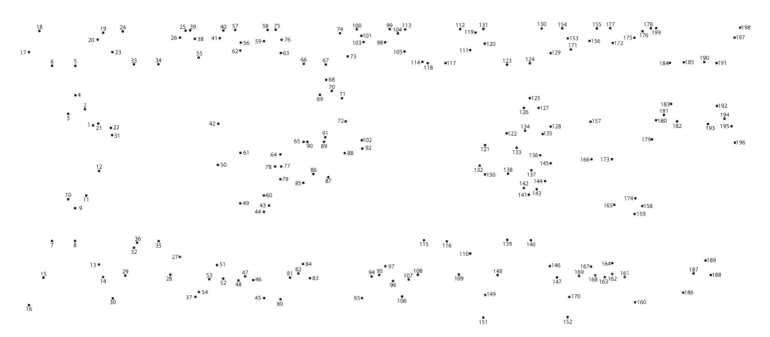

in my

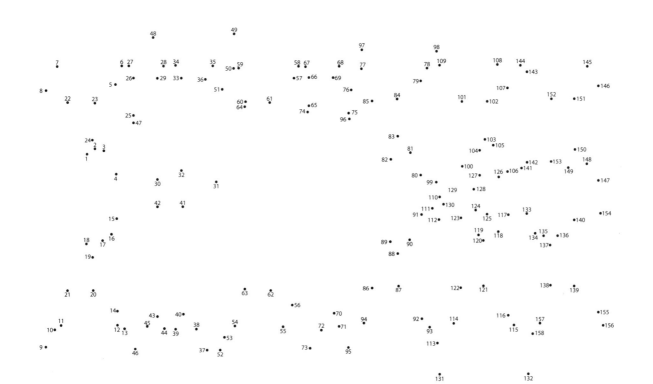

I trust myself and know my inner wisdom is my best guide.

The two most important days in your life are the day you are born and the day you find out why.

Mark Twain

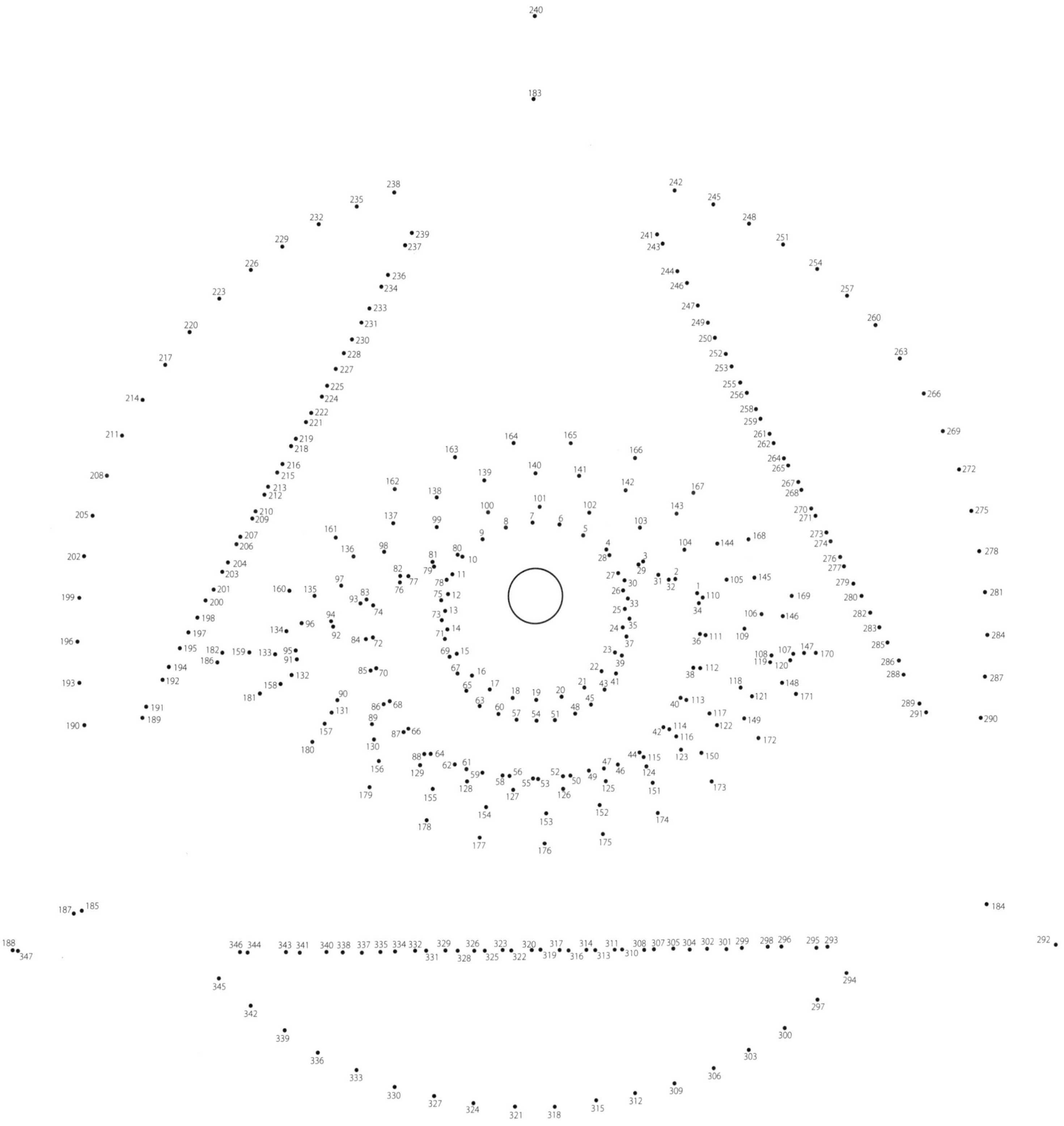

I have integrity — my words
are consistent with my actions.

'Never think that you are not good enough yourself. A man should never think that. People will take you very much at your own reckoning.'

Anthony Trollope

*It's not what you are
that is holding you back.
It's what you think you are not.*

I

to be

with myself

ᏐᏐᏐ

'The opinion which other people have of you is their problem, not yours.'

Elisabeth Kubler-Ross

ᏐᏐᏐ

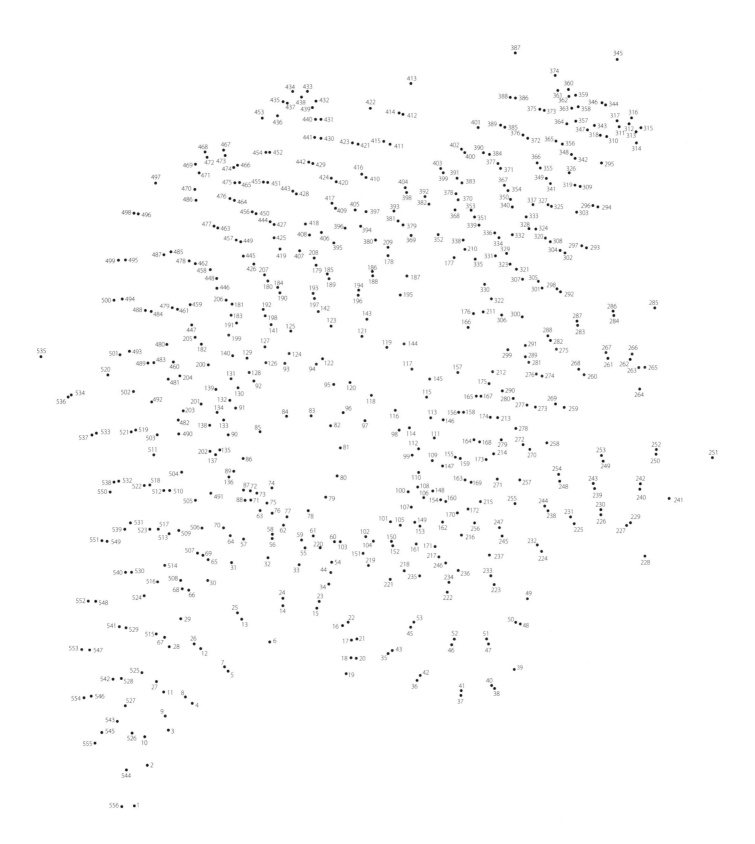

I find deep inner peace
within myself as I am.

I am doing things the

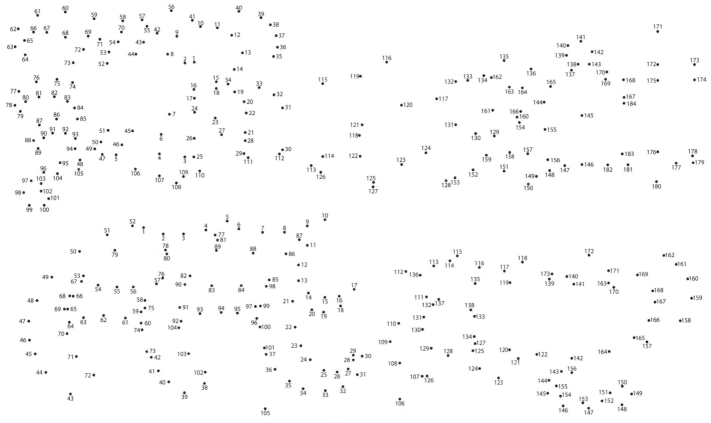

for

'Make voyages.
Attempt them.
There's nothing else.'

Tennessee Williams

I respect my body – I eat healthily and exercise regularly.

§§§

'I have learned over the years that when one's mind is made up, this diminishes fear; knowing what must be done does away with fear.'

Rosa Parks

§§§

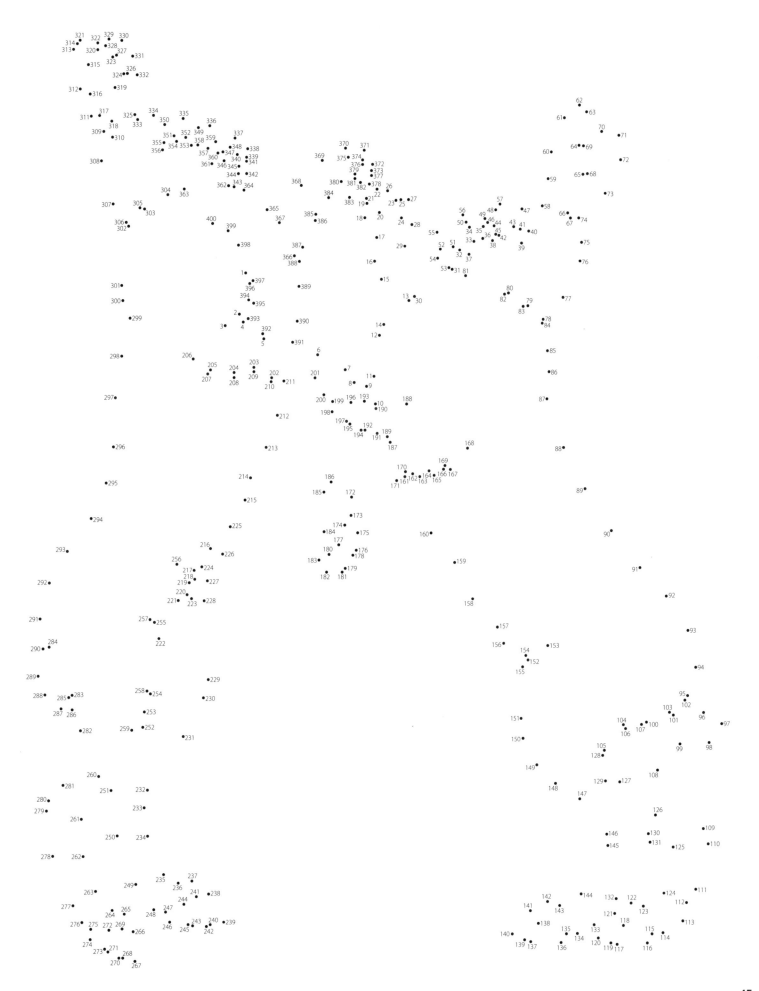

My home is a sanctuary
where I feel safe and happy.

Being

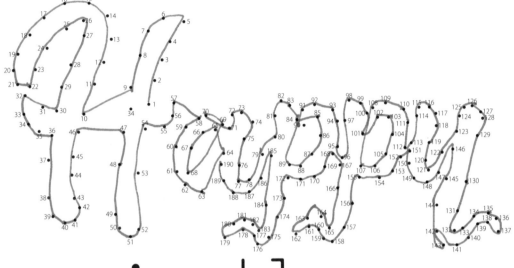

is the

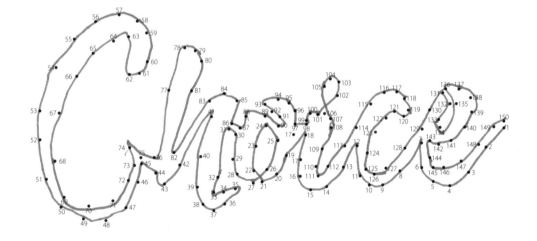

I make today

'Trust yourself.
You know more than
you think you do.'

Benjamin Spock

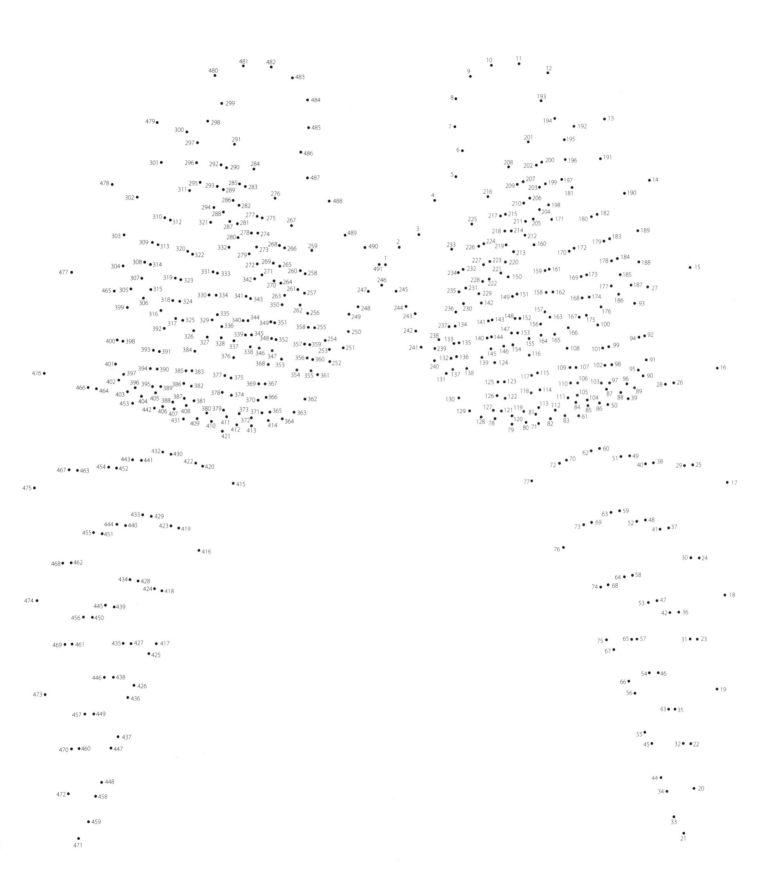

I let go of the past and
live fully in the present moment.

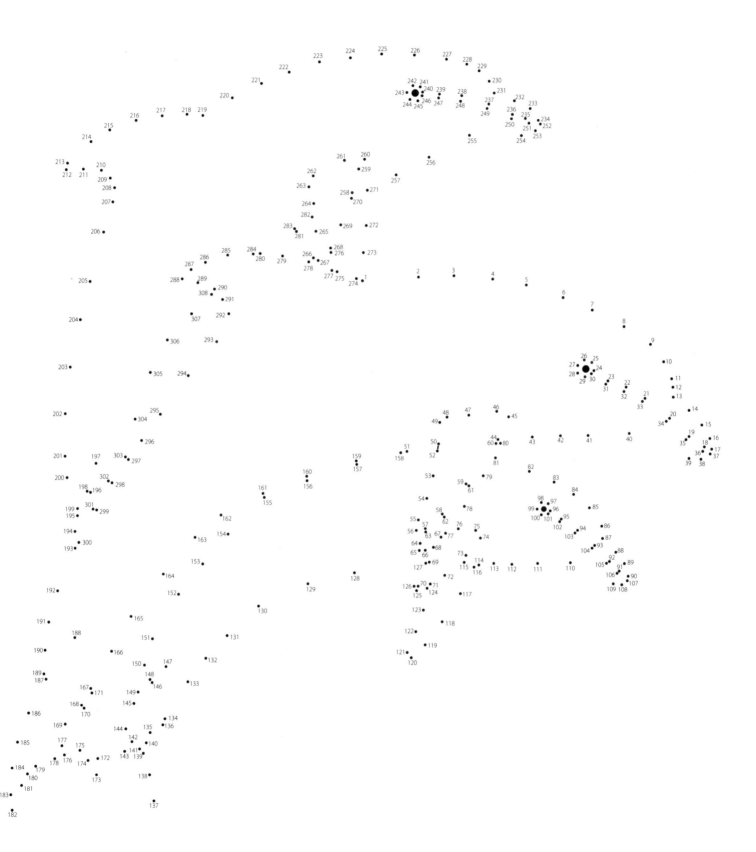

SSS

'Success isn't about
how much money you make.
It's about the difference
you make in people's lives.'

Michelle Obama

SSS

I

my own

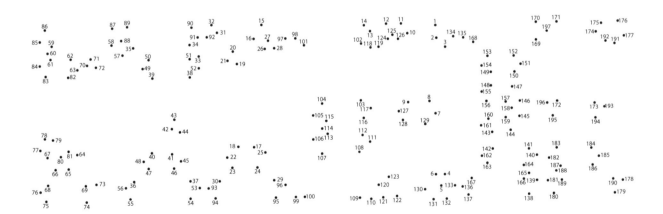

I derive energy from
being calm and relaxed.

'No person has the right
to rain on your dreams.'

Martin Luther King Jr.

I am in charge of how
I feel and today
I am choosing happiness.

My

does not

on the

of others

$\mathcal{SSS}$

'Wanting to be someone else
is a waste of the person you are.'

Marilyn Monroe

$\mathcal{SSS}$

Make yourself a priority
once in a while.
It's not selfish — it's necessary.

'Stay true to yourself.
People respond to authenticity.'

Barbra Streisand

Surround yourself with positive, happy people.

⸙⸙⸙

'What lies behind us and
what lies before us
are tiny matters compared to
what lies within us.'

Ralph Waldo Emerson

⸙⸙⸙

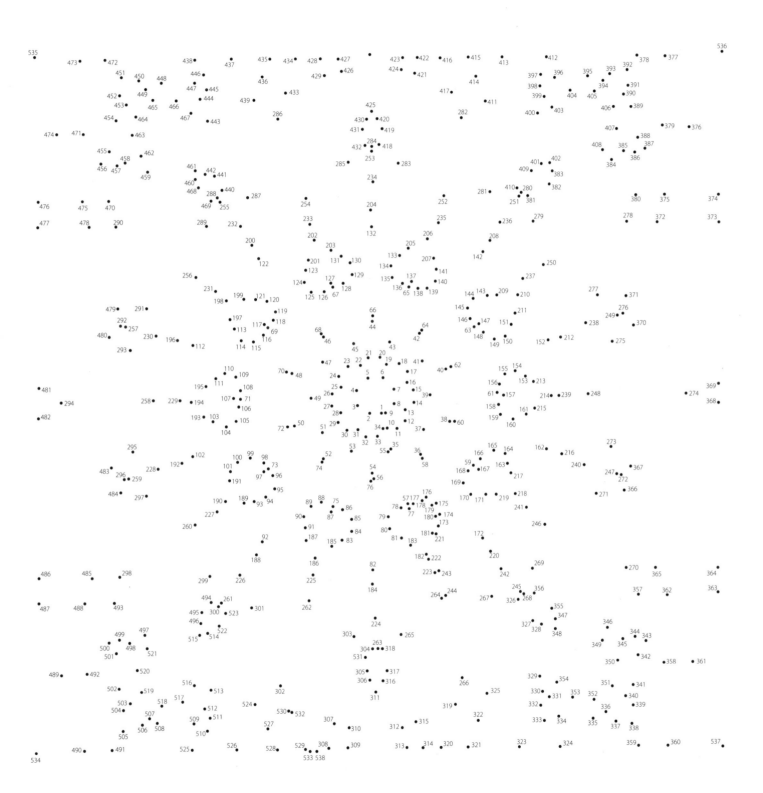

You have to fight through
some bad days to earn
the best days of your life.

I am

than the

I feel

'The thing always happens that you really believe in; and the belief in a thing makes it happen.'

Frank Lloyd Wright

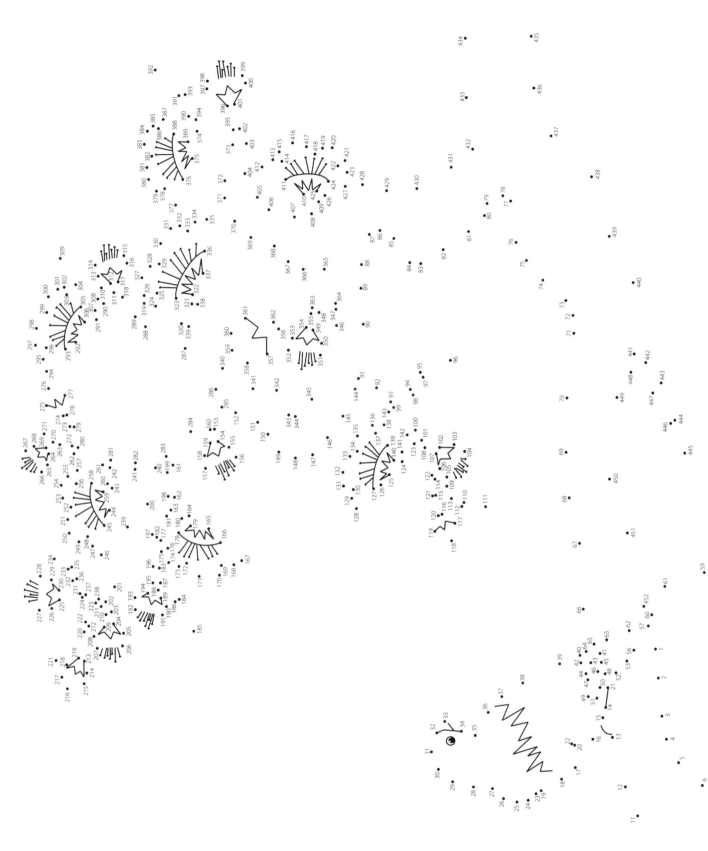

Some see a weed.
I see a wish.

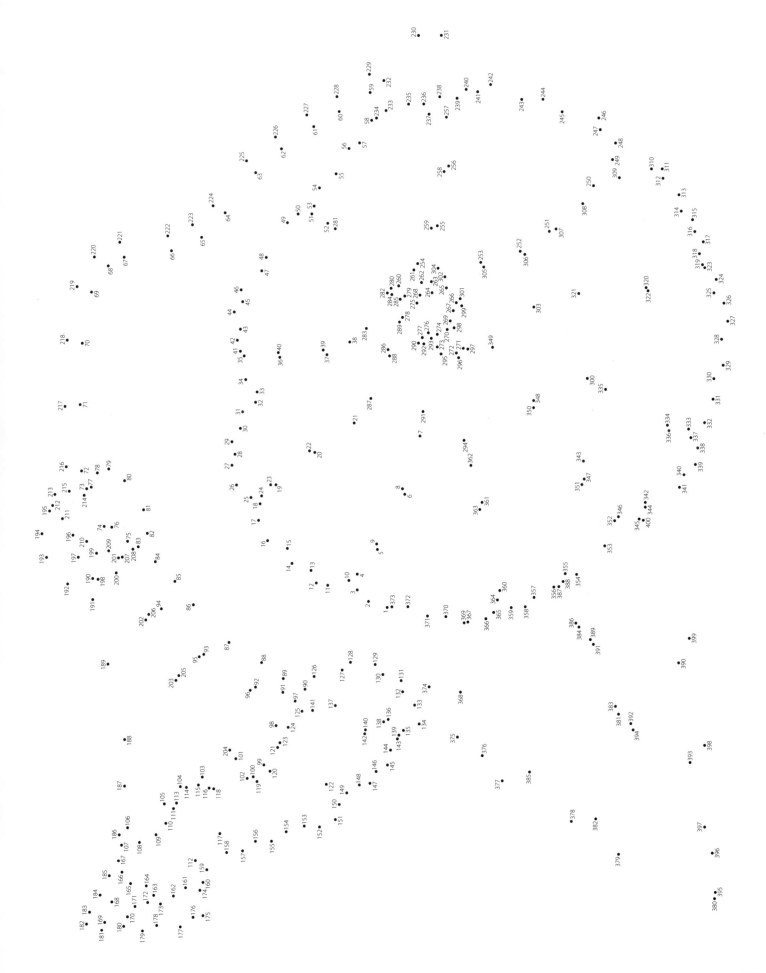

*‘It is good people
who make good places.’*

Anna Sewell

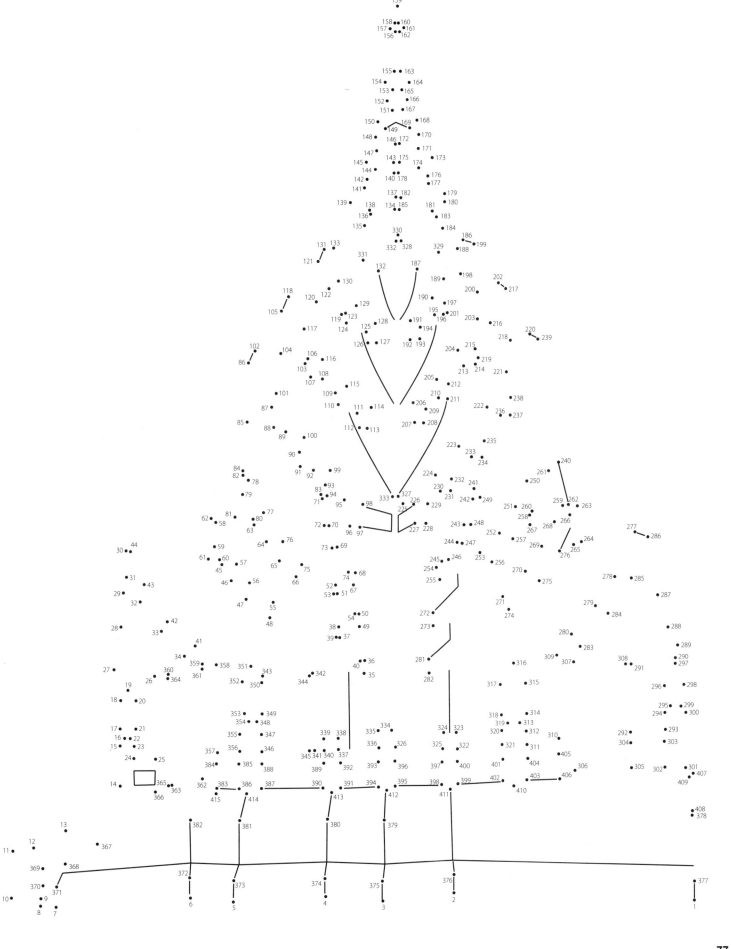

*Beautiful thoughts
and positive emotions are
the stuff miracles are made of.*

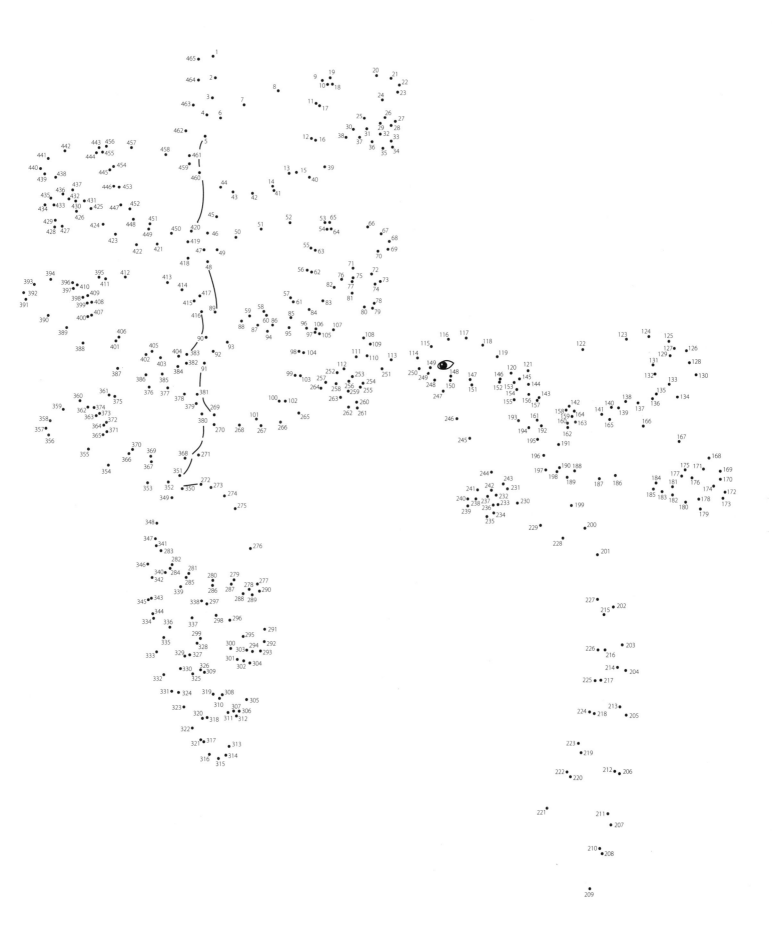

'Impossible is just an opinion.
Don't buy it.'

Robin Sharma

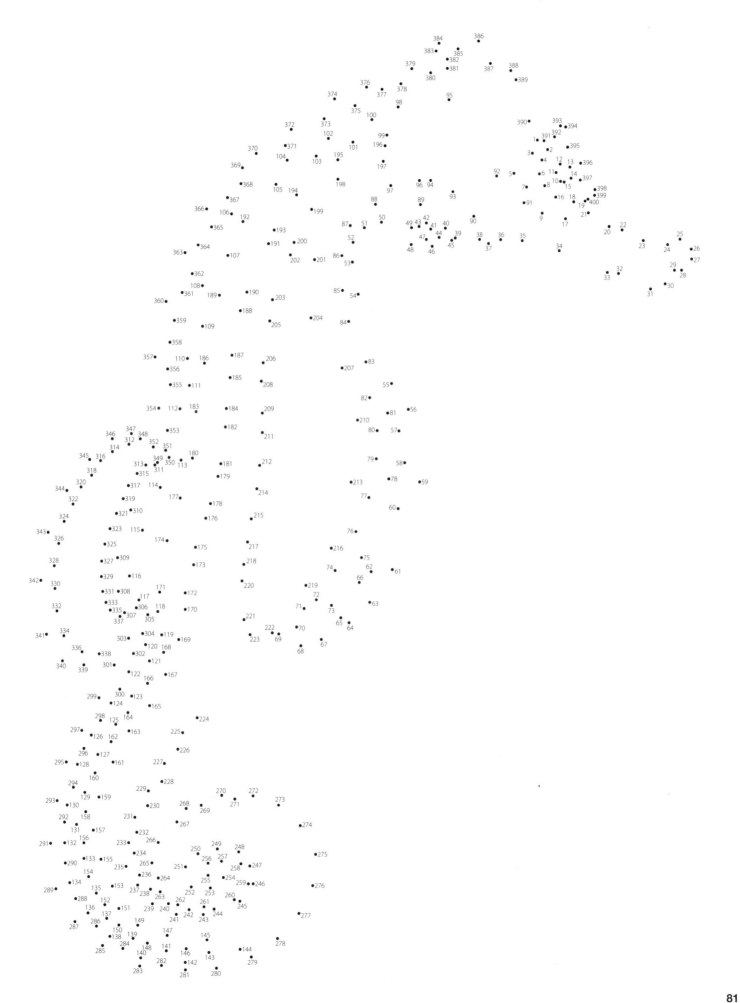

Be the love you wish to see
in the world.

I

to

myself and bring

to others

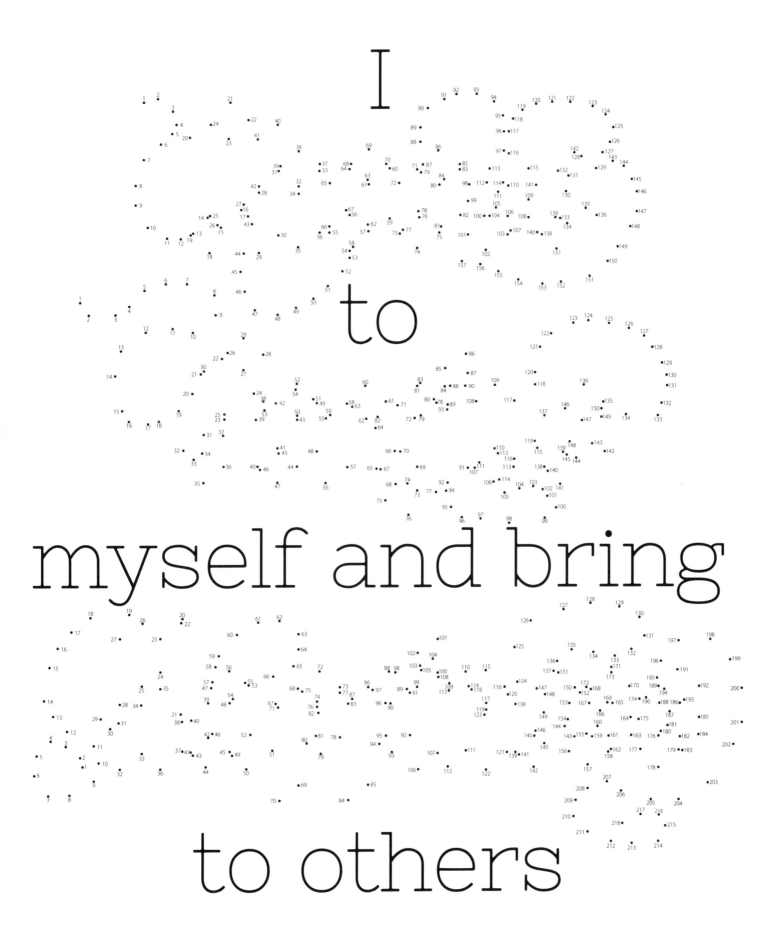

§§§

*'Happiness is the meaning
and the purpose of life,
the whole aim and
end of human existence.'*

Aristotle

§§§

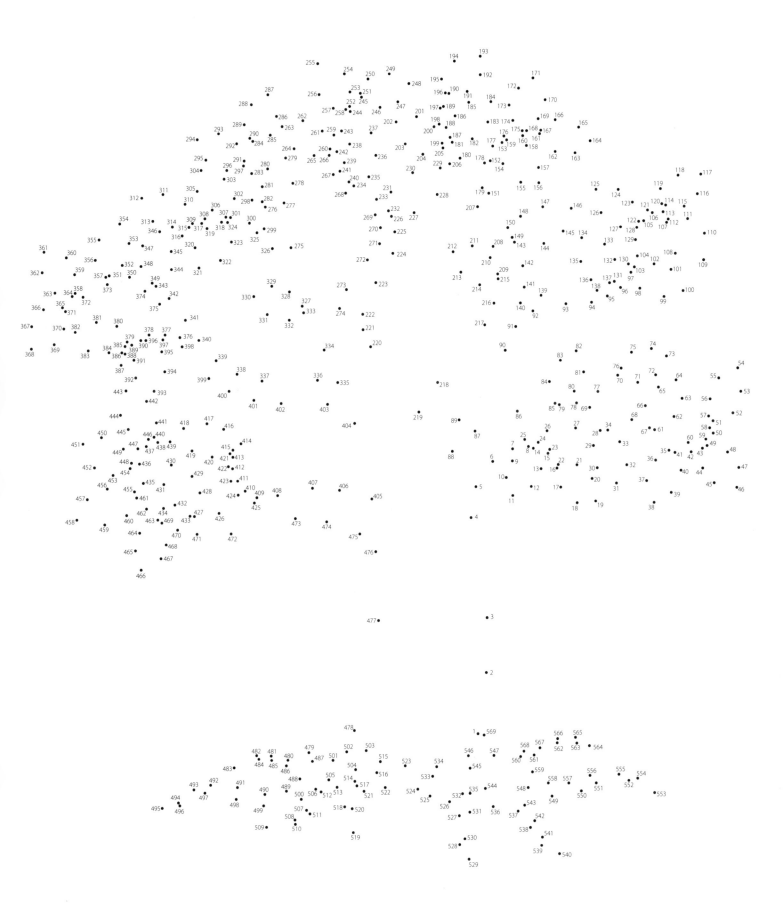

Being positive in a negative situation is not naïve. It's leadership.

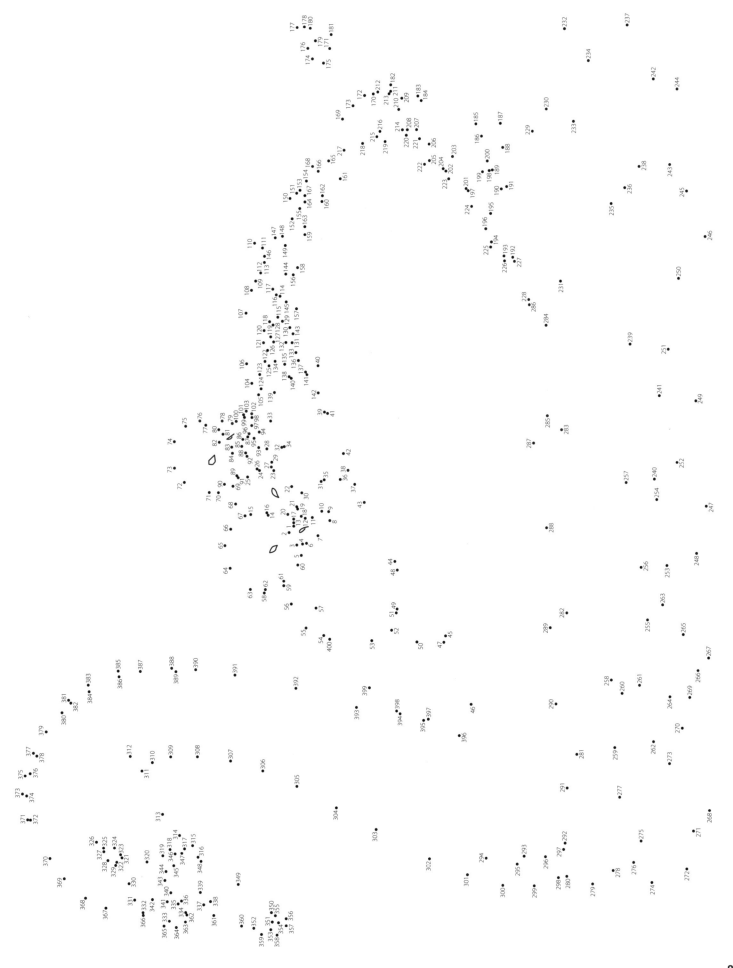

'Be yourself.
No one can say you're
doing it wrong.'

Charles M. Schulz

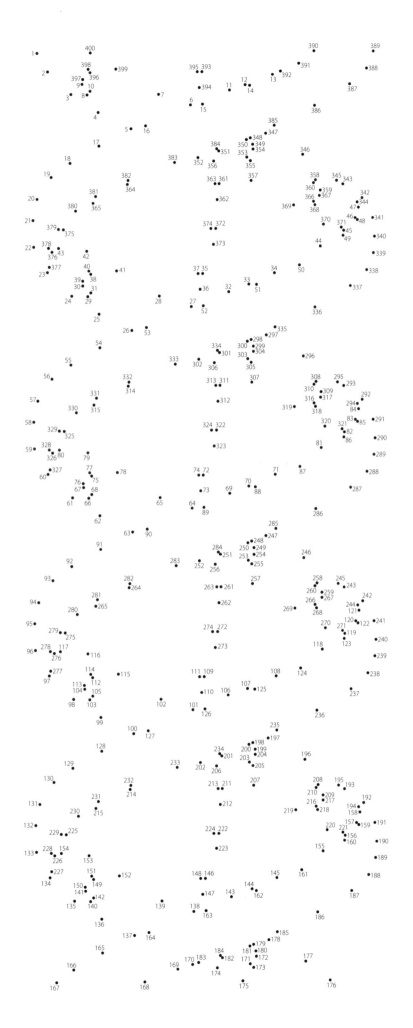

Write it on your heart that every day is the best day in the year.

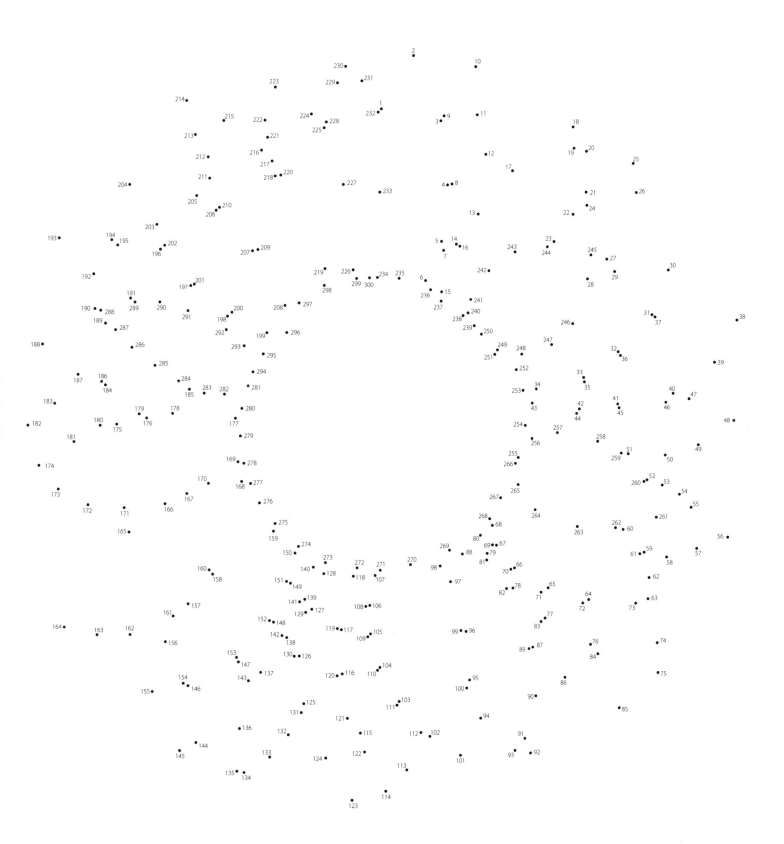

§§§

'The good life is a process,
not a state of being.'

Mark Twain

§§§

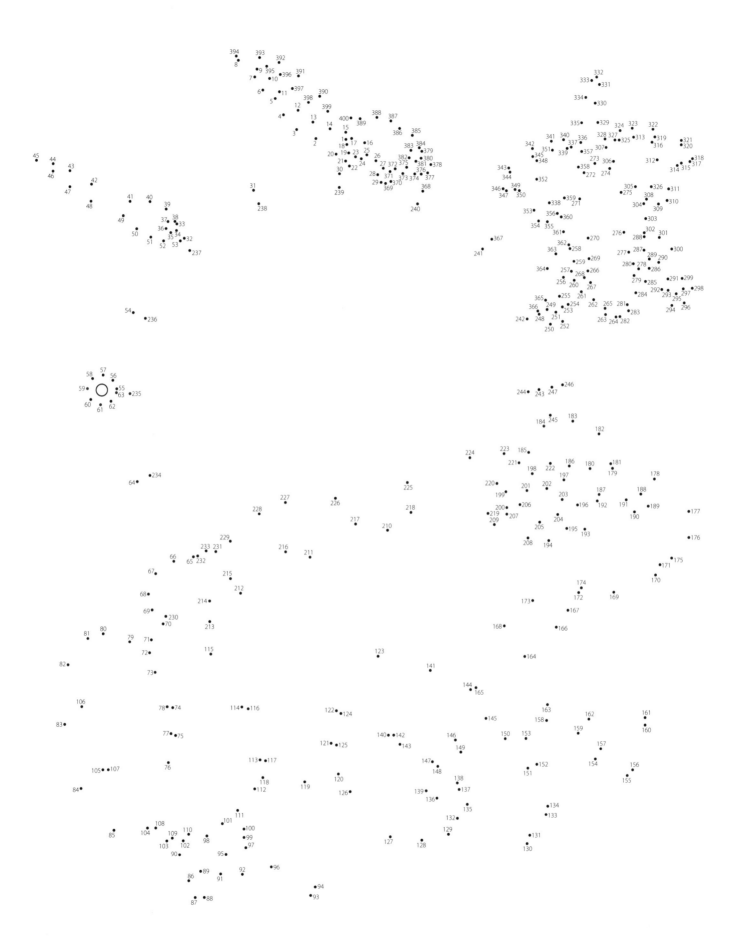

We are all stars
and we deserve to twinkle.

I have enough

and

to meet any

'It's not my responsibility
to be beautiful.
I'm not alive for that purpose.
My existence is not about
how desirable you find me.'

Warsan Shire

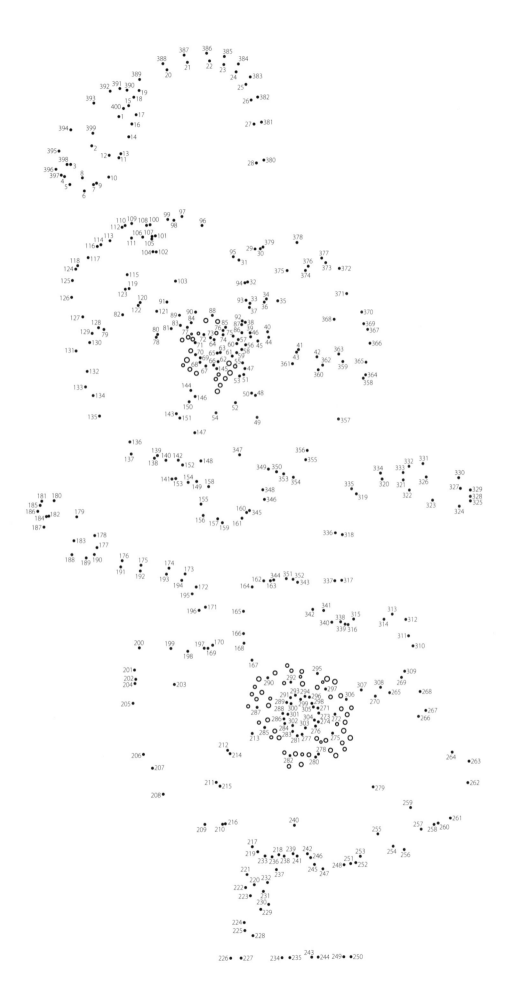

Almost everything will work again

if you unplug it for a while . . .

including you.

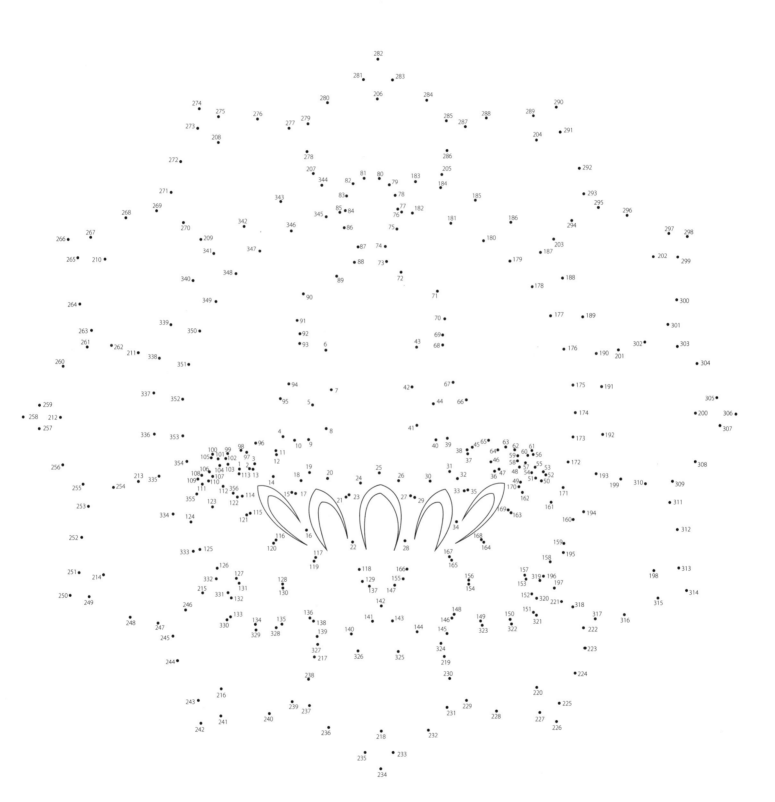

SSS

'The soul always knows
what to do to heal itself.
The challenge is
to silence the mind.'

Caroline Myss

SSS

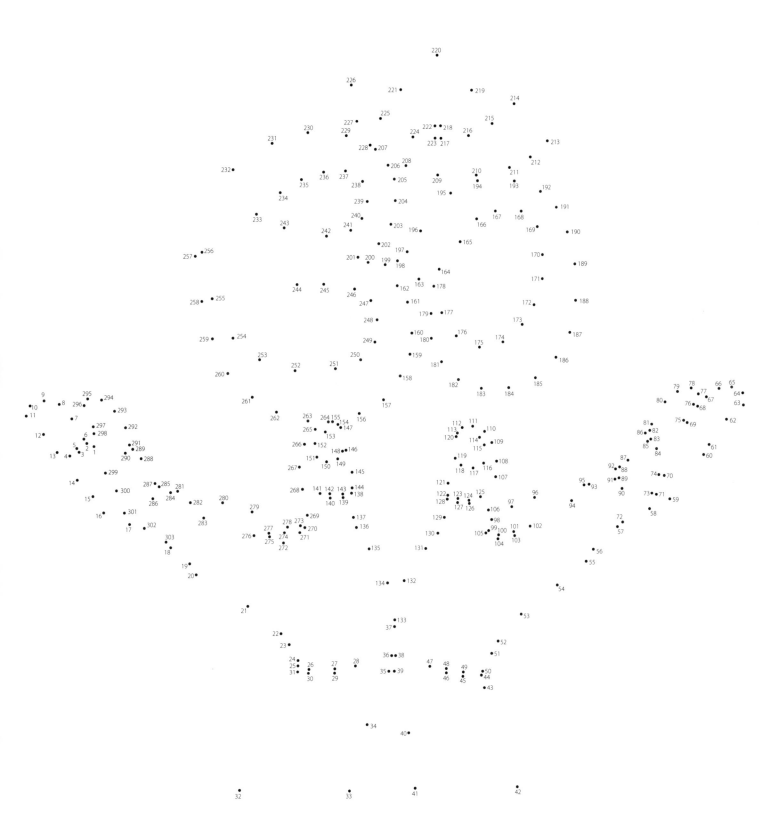

Leadership is not a position or a title, it is action and example.

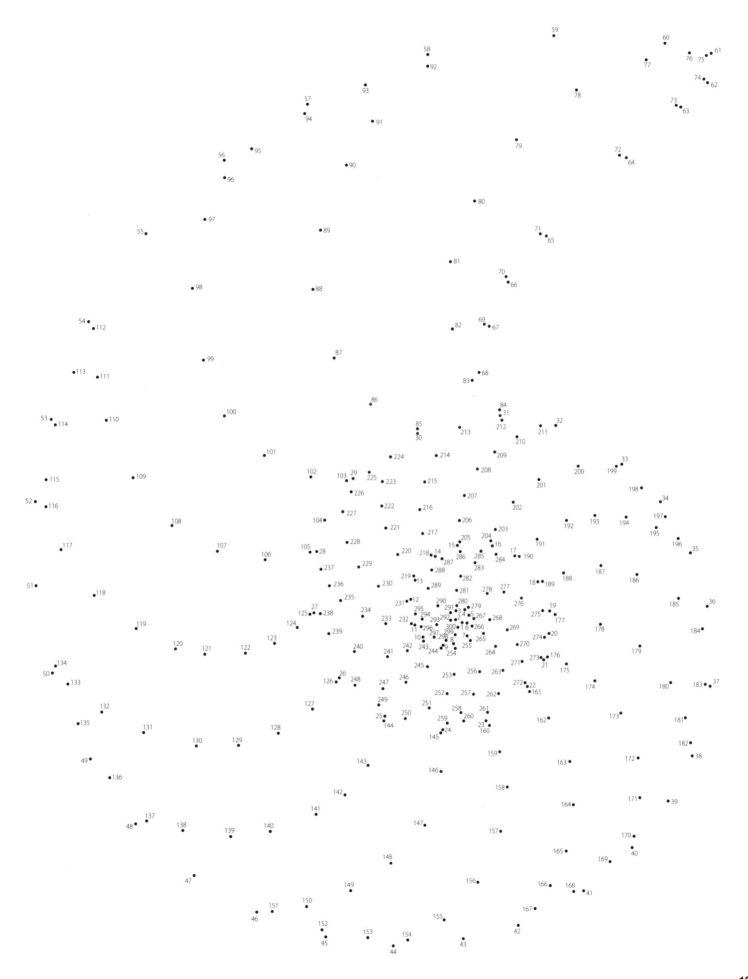

'It is in your moments of decision that your destiny is shaped.'

Tony Robbins

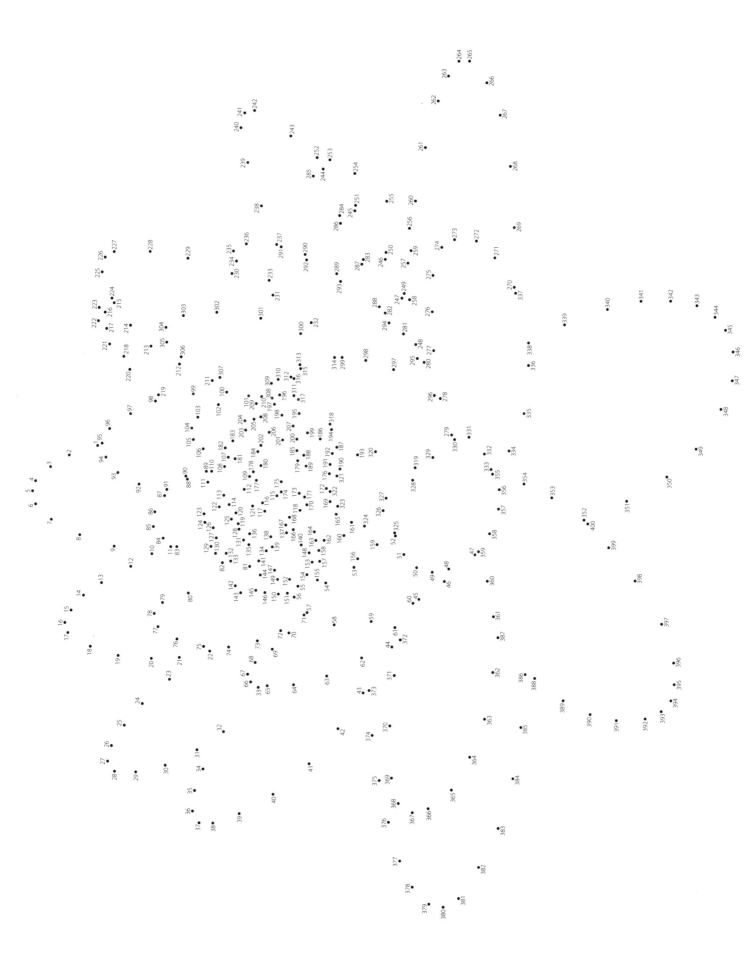

Laugh when you can,
apologize when you should,
and let go of what you can't change.
Life's too short to be anything . . .
but happy.

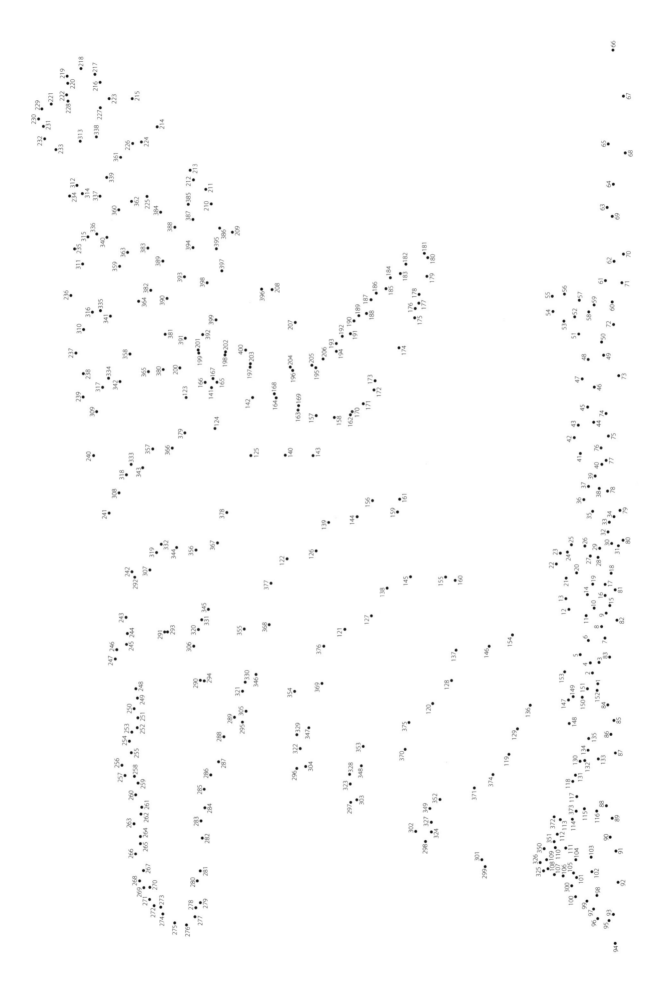

⁂

'No matter who you are,
no matter what you did,
no matter where you've come from,
you can always become
a better version of yourself.'

Madonna

⁂

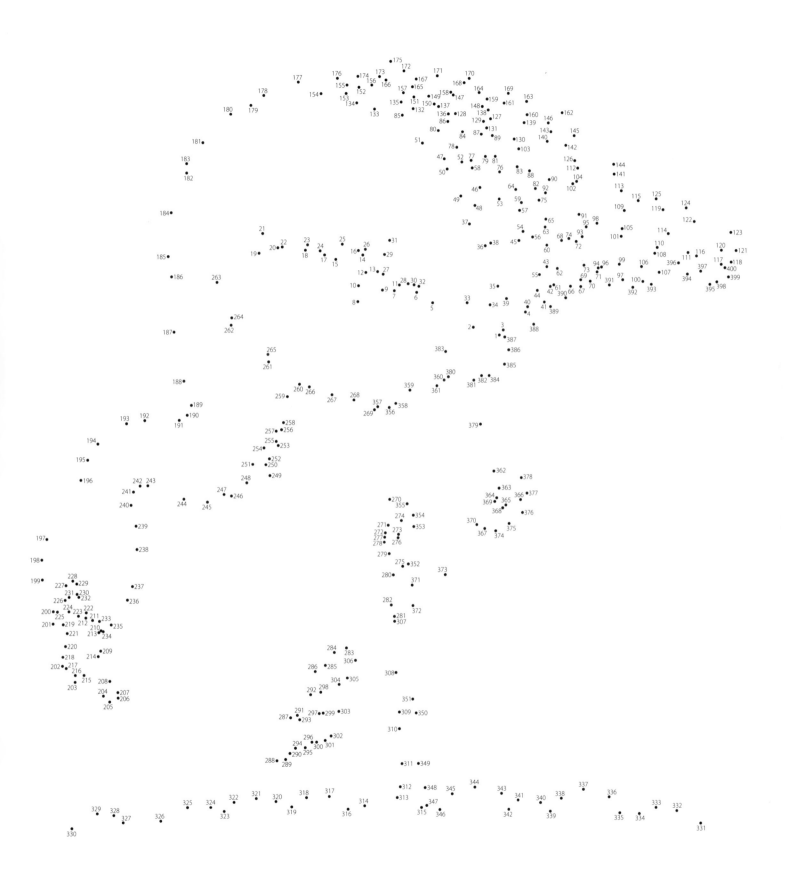

My imperfections make me
unique and special.

'No person is your friend
who demands your silence,
or denies your right to grow.'

Alice Walker

I am

of

and

*A winner is just a loser
who tried one more time.*

'I learned that courage was not
the absence of fear, but the triumph
over it. The brave man is not he
who does not feel afraid,
but he who conquers that fear.'

Nelson Mandela

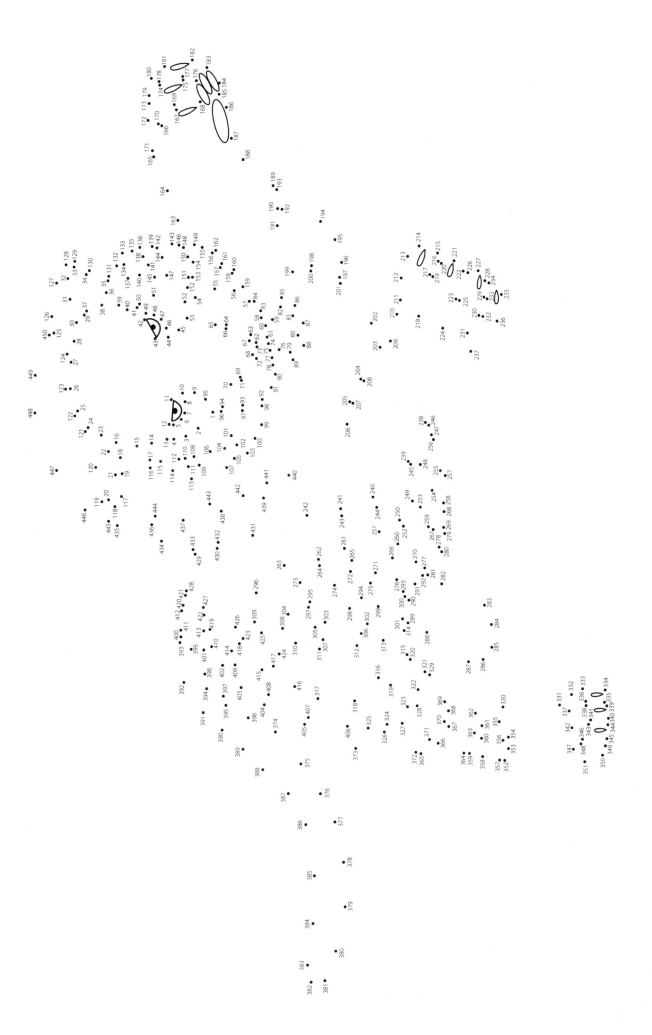

I will face whatever comes today with a positive attitude.

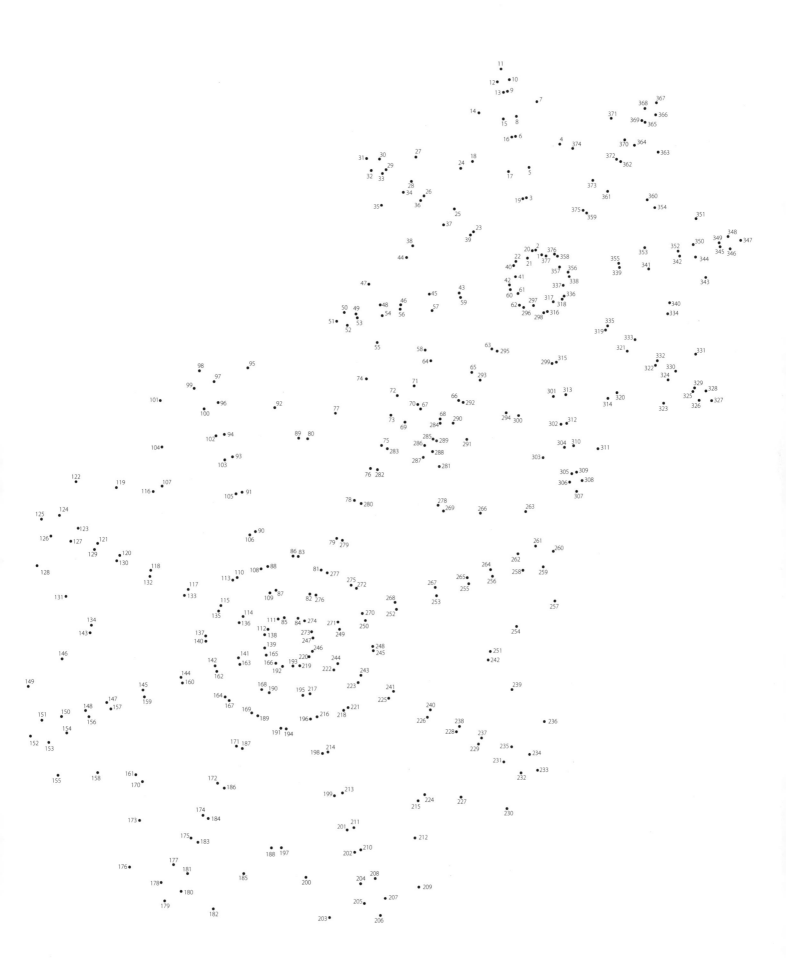

'And those who were seen dancing were thought to be insane by those who could not hear the music.'

Friedrich Nietzsche

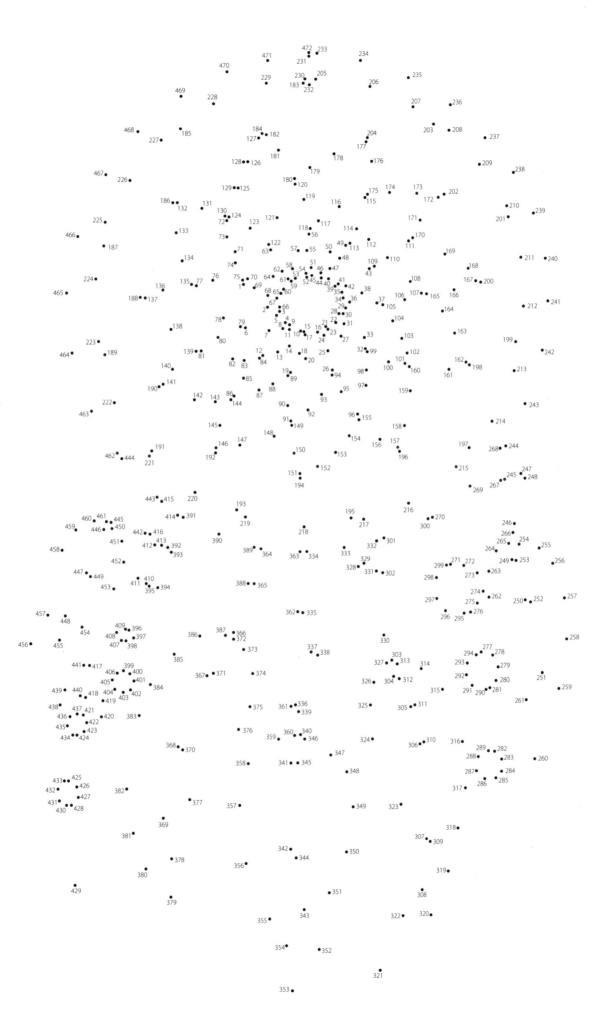

Your mind is a powerful thing.
When you fill it with positive thoughts,
your life will start to change.

I am

to make all the

that I need

The struggle you are in today
is developing the strength
you need for tomorrow.

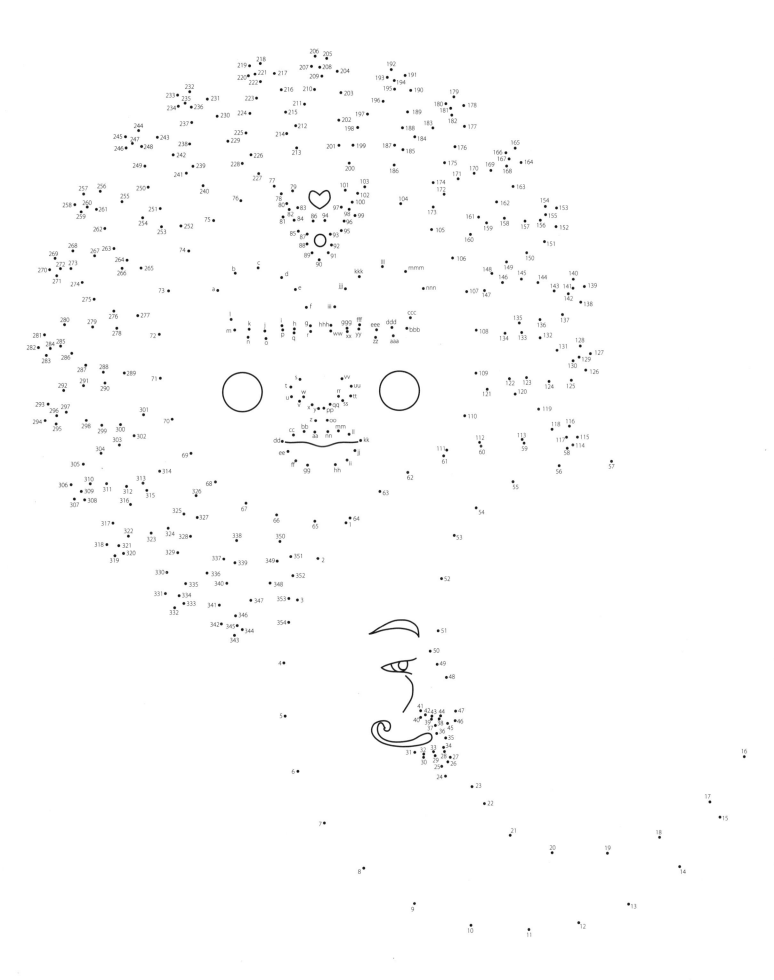

'The final forming of a person's character lies in their own hands.'

Anne Frank

I am

to the

of others

List of images

7 Candles

9 Unicorn

11 Quote: I am supported and I am loved!!!

13 Eye of Horus with lotus flowers

15 Quote: I am valuable and my efforts are enough

17 Celtic knot

19 Quote: I have already accomplished much to be proud of

21 Butterfly landing on a hand

23 Red deer

25 Quote: I am confident in my choices

27 Barn owl

29 All-seeing eye

31 Face of the Buddha

33 Elf maiden with horse

35 Quote: I choose to be patient with myself

37 Peacock feather

39 Quote: I am doing things the best way for me

41 Swallow

43 Woman in standing yoga position

45 Boxing hares

47 Quote: Being happy is the choice I make today

49 Angel wings

51 Dolphins

53 Quote: I appreciate my own journey

55 Bear

57 Dancer

59 Quote: My value does not depend on the approval of others

61 Angel

63 Orchid and spa stones

65 Guardian angel

67 Lotus flower in open hands

69 Islamic tile

71 Quote: I am stronger than the pain I feel

73 Birds on a cherry blossom branch

75 Bindweed

77 Buddhist stupa

79 Hummingbird and flower

81 Seahorse

83 Quote: I choose to forgive myself and bring happiness to others

85 Tree of life

87 Swan and cygnets

89 DNA spiral

91 Sunflower

93 Metamorphosis of frog

95 Quote: I have enough strength and patience to meet any challenge

97 Poppies

99 Meditation

101 OM symbol

103 Fibonacci spiral

105 Water lily

107 Whale breaching

109 Flamingo

111 Duck-billed platypus

113 Quote: I am worthy of respect and love!!

115 Zen garden

117 Tiger

119 Snowflakes

121 Dream catcher

123 Quote: I am ready to make all the changes that I need

125 Sun and moon

127 Quote: I am open to the wisdom of others